This book belongs to

THE WOOLLIES

and

....

To Emily and Arthur, our Aussie imagi-knitters xx —K.M^cK.
To my woollie consultants Harry, Ellie and Meggie —J.S.

OXFORD
UNIVERSITY PRESS

Great Clarendon Street, Oxford OX2 6DP

Oxford University Press is a department of the University of Oxford.
It furthers the University's objective of excellence in research, scholarship,
and education by publishing worldwide.

Oxford is a registered trade mark of Oxford University Press in the UK and in
certain other countries

Text © Oxford University Press 2018
Illustrations © Jon Stuart 2018

The moral rights of the author/illustrator have been asserted Database right
Oxford University Press (maker)

First published in 2018

British Library Cataloguing in Publication Data
Data available

ISBN: 978-0-19-274786-0 (paperback)

10 9 8 7 6 5 4 3 2 1

Printed in China

Paper used in the production of this book is a natural, recyclableproduct made
from wood grown in sustainable forests.The manufacturing process conforms to
the environmental regulations of the country of origin.

'My name's Zip. Today I'm feeling playful!'

'I'm Baby Woolly. I'm the smallest Woolly!'

'Hello, I'm Bling. Do you like my stripy tights?'

'I'm Puzzle. I'm good at sorting things out!'

THE WOOLLIES

Pirates Ahoy!

Kelly McKain
Jon Stuart

OXFORD
UNIVERSITY PRESS

The Woollies were snoozing by their house . . .
Well, all except Baby Woolly.

He spotted a coin in the grass.
'Pirate treasure!' he cried.
'Time for another adventure!'

'I'm off to sail
the seven seas!'

'Ahoy, me hearties!'
Baby Woolly shouted.

'Imagi-knit!'

'. . . my trusty pirate ship!'

Baby Woolly played on his pirate ship. He climbed
the rigging and raised the flag. 'Help, help!'
he cried as he pretended to walk the plank.

Then he sailed away.

Puzzle, Bling, and Zip
heard his shouts.
'Oh no!' gasped Zip. 'Baby
Woolly needs us! Quick!'

'I can't see him anywhere!' cried Puzzle.
'Let's go and find him!' said Bling.
'Imagi-knit!'

They looked above
the water . . .

. . . and below the water.
But there was no sign of Baby Woolly.

'I'll put the periscope all the way up so we can see where we are,' said Zip.

'We must be brave and keep looking for Baby Woolly,' Puzzle said.

'I don't like this!' said Bling, trembling.

'Shiver me timbers, me hearties, it's a pirate's life for me!' laughed Baby Woolly as he sailed around the island.

'What's that lurking under the water?' wondered Baby Woolly. He started to feel very scared.

The thing reared its head. 'Argh! A sea monster!' cried Baby Woolly. 'Hang on, it's knitted! My friends must be down there. I think they need my help!'

'But where is my backpack?
Oh no, it's gone! How can I imagi-knit?'

Then Baby Woolly had an idea.
'I know, I'll make a wish on my lucky
pirate coin,' he said. 'I wish, I wish . . .
my woolly backpack would come back!'

Suddenly, it did.
'My wish came true!'
gasped Baby Woolly.
'No time to lose. Imagi-knit!'

'Baby Woolly to the rescue!' he mumbled.

He cut his woolly friends free . . .

The Woollies all cheered.
'Hip hip hooray for
Baby Woolly!'

'You saved us, Baby Woolly!' Zip said.
'Thank you!'
'You're welcome,' Baby Woolly yawned.
It had been a big, busy adventure.
'Come on, let's go home,' said Bling.
'Even pirates need their naps.'

'Happy snoozing, Baby Pirate!'

A note for grown-ups

Oxford Owl is a FREE and easy-to-use website packed with support and advice about everything to do with reading.

Informative videos

Hints, tips and fun activities

Top tips from top writers for reading with your child

Help with choosing picture books

For this expert advice and much, much more about how children learn to read and how to keep them reading ...

LOOK
for Oxford Owl
www.oxfordowl.co.uk